GW00746092

CHARLES CLARKE continues from Suffolk Signs Book 2
Suffolk's most prolific sign makers, the late Harry Carter of '
Hector) of Brandeston Forge, assisted by Mr. Terry Pearce of .

THE FAMOUS HARRY CARTER SIGNS

Before any design could be contemplated, Mr. Carter spent many hours in libraries, seeking historical or legendary stories and characters to be incorporated into a sign. He preferred to choose a piece of history unique to the parish concerned, so research was vital. He then produced one or two design ideas to discuss with the sponsors, who might have their own suggestions to make. However, normally it was left to Harry to make the final decision and design.

Once agreed, the action started! Apparently the biggest problem for a carved wooden sign is the choice of wood. Seasoned timber is essential. His early work was carried out in oak but he has since used maghogany and cedar. It has been said that he carved like a medieval craftsman, often using tools that he had designed and made himself. He had a bold style that he considered appropriate for work that must withstand all weathers. The facets left by the chisel help to dispel the rain, although the whole carving was preserved in yacht varnish. It could take months of work for a sign to be completed, but in spite of this, Harry only charged for the materials, the undoubted reason why the region is so rich in village signs. Due to failing eyesight, he had to make the Suffolk village of Sproughton the proud owner of his last sign, a truly magnificent example of his work. (Featured in Suffolk Signs Book 2.)

BRANDESTON FORGE METAL SIGNS

In the majority of cases, representatives from the village requesting a new sign bring ideas and Mrs. Mary Moore compiles these into two or three suitable designs. Coloured scale drawings and estimates are prepared. Once the design is chosen, Mrs. Moore draws it out full size. Working directly in plaster, strengthened with wood and metal, she models the pictorial patterns in relief, on one or both sides as required. The lettering panels are prepared in the same way, usually with hand-cut letters. These panels, known as the patterns, are then sent to L. C. Jay Ltd., of Norwich, who produce replicas in cast aluminium. Meanwhile the wrought-iron work, i.e. frame, decorative scrollwork, brackets, etc., is forged in the workshop, again working from full-sized drawings. When they are returned, the cast aluminium panels are hand-finished and prepared for fitting. Metal primer and white undercoat is applied, before Mary's final painting and gilding. Everything is finally assembled and fitted to the prepared post, usually made from fresh cut oak. Hector Moore, assisted by Terry Pearce of Bredfield Forge, has always tried to make the wrought-iron work interesting and unique. with unusual scrolls, scroll ends and finials. Each sign designed by Mary Moore has at least one example of animal or bird life, however insignificant and not always noticed until the sign is finished. (The bat in her own village sign, featured in Suffolk Signs Book 2, is a case in point.) The Moore signs continue to make their own distinctive mark on village sign production. This book contains two new ones, at Great Blakenham and Saxmundham, both with unique touches.

GREAT BLAKENHAM

Gt. Blakenham, a recent sign coming from Brandeston Forge, is a beautiful example of the work of Mary & Hector Moore. Shield-shaped, with sturdy black wrought-iron scrolling by Terry Pearce of Bredfield Forge, it is colourful and attractive, especially the name plate, forming the cross pieces of the 'shield'. Scrolled and tasselled, these cross pieces meet at the common 'E' of GrEat BlakEnham, fortunately for the design, being the central letter of each word.

The village, past and present, is depicted, with the Church, complete with War Memorial and Churchyard, the ancient Parish Room, the Bridge and the hens denoting Brands Chicken factory, a source of local employment.

Great Blakenham was a typical sleepy Suffolk village until the railway arrived in 1846. 'Claydon' station is actually in Gt. Blakenham and most of the industry was built on the boundary of the two villages, standing alongside the old Ipswich to Bury St. Edmunds road.

The top left hand panel of the 'shield' celebrates the rural aspect, with large trees, fields and houses, with the tall chimney of the cement works, another source of local employment, towering above, as it has done for a century or more.

The top right-hand panel has an attractive painting of the Church, churchyard and War Memorial. The simple church has items of interest, including a beautifully carved Jacobean pulpit, an ancient octagonal font, with emblems of the Passion and a sacred heart. There is the tomb of Richard Swift, complete with kneeling angels. Swift was a London merchant in the mid-17th. century. Norman remains are embodied in the newer parts of the church. There was a Benedictine cell in the village of the Monastery of Bec, which was removed by Henry VI. Eton College has held the manor of Great Blakenham ever since it was conferred on it in ancient times.

The panel below shows the Parish Room, 100 years old, but now disused. It had been the meeting place for the village since 1897. The W.I. held meetings there for 80 years. The strutting hens remind us of the Brand factory, giving employment to the village.

The lower left hand panel shows the river and the bridge. This once had a mill beside it, where barges passed through from Stowmarket to Ipswich docks. It was burned down early this century.

The sign, which stands on Hackney's Corner, is mounted on a sturdy post, set in a plinth generously given to the village by Mike & Wendy Wootten. Mike also designed parts of the shield. The finished work is an amalgam of various ideas, drawings and shapes submitted in a village W.I. competition to design a sign. It was unveiled by the oldest residents, Mrs. Cardy and Mr. Gooding and dedicated by the vicar, the Rev. Nina Brown. A plaque helps visitors to appreciate the sign.

Mary Moore with the sign in her workshop
Great Blakenham sign
Terry Pearce at work on Framlingham sign
Saxmundham unveiling: L to R. Terry Pearce, Roger Peace, Jenny Toombs and Mary Moore

OUSDEN

The sign at Ousden, erected on October 26th. 1996, was given to the village by Roy and Doreen Claydon, because of their long association there. It is one of the most attractive, designed and made by Brian Gaze. Double-sided, with each side very slightly different, it shows both sides of the Church, with a large owl in flight above. One side shows the church porch and lych gate, the other the tombstones. Both have wildlife in the foreground, with poppies, daisies and other wild flowers to the side. Sheaves of corn and 2 rabbits complete the scene.

More trees and foliage frame the picture, topped by the name-plate arched above. The sign stands on the Green, in front of a beautiful thatched cottage. The owls are accentuated because Ousden, Uuesdana in the Domesday Book, means place of owls. The quaint little Norman church has a door half Norman half early English. The chancel is under the tower, which has impressive round Norman arches, with grey flintwork and contrasting mellow stone. There is a lofty font, supported on its 9 columns for over 500 years. (Cover picture by Ian Craig. Reverse, P.6, S. Addy)

DALHAM

The sign at Dalham, on the B1085 near Newmarket, stands before a thatched cottage, beside the bridge over the River Kennet. Harry Carter of Swaffham designed it for the Silver Jubilee of Queen Elizabeth II. It shows four principal village landmarks: St. Mary's Church is in the central background, minus its spire, which fell down in storms on the day that Oliver Cromwell died. To the left is the 50 foot tall windmill, still in good repair. There are the maltings, with a conical roof and the river in the foreground. Thatched cottages complete the picture.

Francis and Cecil Rhodes lived here, in the Hall, once occupied by Wellington. Francis built the village hall and restored the church roof as a memorial to Cecil when he died in Africa. Francis died there too in 1905, at Cecil's house, not far from his brother's grave. He was brought home and buried here, aged 54, and a plaque to commemorate him reads: *Long travels in this churchyard end A gentleman who knew no fear. A soldier, sportsman, Prince of friends, A man men could but love, lies here.* The nearby Affleck Arms public house reminds us that the 18th. C. Admiral, Sir Edmund Affleck, distinguished in skirmishes with the French, is thought to be buried here in the family vault. Over the chancel arch, in the church, are traces of an old painting of The Last Judgement, with a huge devil's head by another arch, representing one of the Seven Deadly Sins.

HINDERCLAY

Spelt as Hilderclea in the Domesday Book, meaning 'tongue of land where there are elder trees', Hinderclay lies near the A143 Bury St. Edmunds to Diss road. Its sign, another beautiful example manufactured by Brian Gaze, was unveiled by Colonel David Pudney, Lord of the Manor, on October 13th. 1990.

Designed by Karen Calton, the sign shows the church, the village mill, sheaves of corn, with oak leaves, acorns and wheat stalks, as well as a 'Gotch' jug, historically filled with ale for the bellringers. The original was made in 1724 and is now in Bury St. Edmunds' Museum. The church is an architectural gem, with a tiered tower and contrasting porch. It has low plastered barrel ceilings. The place-name is white on a blue sash background and this delicately-coloured attractive sign shows leaves and daisies in the foreground. The sign is mounted on black wrought-iron scrollwork.

SAXMUNDHAM

Saxmundham, named in the Domesday book as Sasmundeham, meaning 'homestead of a man named Seaxel', is a thriving market town, on the old turnpike road from London to Gt. Yarmouth, now bypassed by the A12. Its attractive sign, dedicated to 50 years of peace, was planned for 1995, but technicalities and problems with siting delayed it until the summer of 1997. It was erected in July by local builder Graham Smith, but presented to the townspeople by Stephen Palmer, representing the Parish Council, on Sept. 28th., when it was dedicated by the Rural Dean, Canon Roger Smith. He quoted from the book of Amos, 'Let justice roll on like a river and righteousness like a never-failing stream'. then spoke and prayed for peace between the nations, in business, community and family life and for the victims of war and suffering. Praise was given to God the King of all nations, and Christ, the Prince of Peace. Thanks were given for deliverance from danger, for the lives lost in wars, for those who promote and pursue peaceful ways. The large crowd attending were urged to dedicate themselves to peace.

The Leiston Royal British Legion Band played marches and songs from the war years, finally leading the Parish Council members and uniformed organisations back to the historic Market Hall, where Roy Simpson spoke of steering the sign through the necessary procedures until his last task of screwing the bronze dedicatory plaque to the post!

Designed by Jenny Toombs, of Benhall, from 30 drawings submitted by local children from Saxmundham Primary and Middle Schools, encouraged by Roy Simpson, (Parish Council) the sign is shield-shaped, in cast aluminium, with a black wrought iron frame and dove of peace at the top. The bottom half has a striking reproduction of the ancient Market Hall. There has been a market here since it was granted in 1272. It occupied a seven-acre site in 1311. The impressive facaded Hall, presented to the town by the Long family, was built in 1842-6, with the Corn Hall and the rebuilding of the Bell Inn, then refurbished in 1992. The arms of the Longs of Hurts Hall (to the south of the town and rebuilt in 1890 by Cotman) are proudly displayed as well as a public clock and the patriotic motto, *Dieu et ma Patra.*

The top two quarters of the sign depict, to the left, two sheep and a cow, denoting the agricultural aspects and the ancient cattle market, with fencing used as the spandrels of the sign to reinforce the idea. The right-hand side has a painting of the much restored church. Thomas Thurlow is buried in the churchyard and his monumental work is in evidence in the interior, as well as that of Nollekens, and Westmacott. The south chancel, 1308, has nine beautiful panels of Flemish glass.

The master pattern from Jenny's design was made by Mary & Hector Moore with Terry Pearce at Brandeston Forge.

Roger Peace, of Jays Foundry, Norwich, was responsible for casting the main panel from the master pattern, and the bronze dedicatory plaque which is fixed to the sign's sturdy Suffolk oak post.

The black wrought iron frame, dove, bottom supports, etc.,were manufactured by Terry Pearce of Bredfield Forge, in conjunction with the Moores.

The nameplate is incorporated at the base of the shield, with striking black letters on white, framed in gold and black.

This attractive sign is sited on the B1121 from Kelsale, on the pavement on the left, just under the railway bridge.

ASHLEY

The village name means 'ash tree wood or clearing'. The village sign stands on a green just off the B1063 from Newmarket to Clare, in front of the ancient horse pond. The pond railings are depicted on the sign, in front of a large ash tree.

This attractively simple black wrought iron sign was designed by Ashley Art group and made by Peter Bridge, husband of its leader.

The village name is arched boldly across in gold leaf, with the stars of the De Vere family, Earls of Oxford, in gold below. The family held Silverley, the tiny hamlet adjoining Ashley, which now has only half a dozen homesteads. The ruined tower of Silverley Abbey, (found on the B1063 to Clare) is depicted to the right of the Ash tree, with the bell tower of Ashley Parish Church of St. Mary to the left.

The central cross of St. John celebrates the association of the Knights Hospitallers, with the village.

The sign commemorates the Centenary of the Parish Council in 1994, with 'A.P.C'. within an embracing C on the post, cut from one piece of metal by Peter Bridge. The sign stands on a flat black studded base and was unveiled on V.E. Day, May 1995.

BARNHAM

Just off the A134, south of Thetford, is Barnham, spelt c.1000 as Byornham, 'homestead of a man called Beorn'. Its unusual sign, with collage-type cut-outs on a blue background, feature the old mill, no longer working, with an aeroplane above a steam train, pulling a trailer carrying two sheep. The plane is a R.A.F. Tornado from nearby Honnington.

There was an old forge years back, which is not shown and two churches, suggesting former populance. St. Martins has nothing left but a ruined tower, whereas smaller St. Gregory's has a Victorian air, but possesses a 13th.C. font and an exceptionally fine piscena with tracery above lovely shafts. Thatched cottages sit comfortably with the landscape. A piece of a carved Anglo-Saxon coffin lid is built into a flint cottage north of the Churchyard.

The sign was made by Mr. Ian Clark and unveiled by the Countess of Euston.

BRANDON

In the 11th. C. spelt as Bromdun, meaning 'hill where broom grows', Brandon is N.W. of Thetford on the Suffolk/Norfolk border. The sign is near the B1107-A1065 roundabout. It takes the form of a wooden 'T', with black wrought-iron spandrels and surrounding scrollwork. A colourful semi-circular panel above shows men flint-knapping, a highly skilled and ancient craft. The place-name is in black lettering in a band above.

Brandon has always been well-known for its flint. A working site lies behind the Flintmakers Arms, an Elizabethan inn near the sign. The entire village is mainly built of flint and it was exported, Brandon being the port of Thetford until the River Little Ouse extended upwards.

Flints have been dug up out of Grimes Graves by Neolithic men, who found them in layers less than a foot thick and as deep as 30 feet underground in the underlying chalk. Flint has probably been mined here from around 10,000 B.C.

Although not a rabbit to be seen on the sign, Burstall was also rich in the fur trade. Both have now given way to forestry as the main source of income. Brandon House Hotel was the home of leading furriers, the Rought-Roughts. Brandon Staunch, half a mile west, is one of 7 lock gates erected by Thetford Corporation in 1829. The village was granted the right to markets and fairs in 1319. The church, on a pre-Norman site shows features from 13th.C. onwards. Brandon Park has been a Country Park since 1973, but Knapper Way and Warren Close pay tribute to their ancient wealth.

BURSTALL

Burstall lies just off the B1071, west of Ipswich. Its spelling in the Domesday Book was Burgestala, 'site of a fort'.

It has a magnificent sign, made in 1989 by Mary and Hector Moore of Brandeston Forge. It was unveiled by Mr. Robin Cousins, who spent much time and effort on the project.

Shield-shaped, with a central horizontal bar, the coat of arms of Henry VIII takes centre place, topped with a plaque of white lilies on a blue background. To the left is the unusual clock tower, with the Church of St. Mary the Virgin on the right. Below is the Cranfield Memorial Hall, named after and given to the village in 1910 by the well-known Ipswich milling family. Trees and greenery enhance the whole scene and the scrolled place-name is on a gold banner below, with blue lettering. A black wrought-iron frame and spandrels complete this meaningful, colourful and historical sign.

In 1528 Henry VIII granted the manor of Harrolds in Burstall to Cardinal Wolsey, to help finance Wolsey's college in Ipswich. The project was never completed and only the gateway stands, in St. Peter's St. It is said that the coat of arms found over the mantlepiece in Mulberry Hall was put there by the Cardinal to show his allegiance to the crown, but it is not known if he ever lived there or visited the Hall.

The church is a gem, with a splendid 14th.C. screen, fine 15th.C. hammerbeam roof, lovely traceried windows, old and newer, and in 1795 a vicar, George Naylor, served for 59 years there.

BRUISYARD

The village lies in pastureland and its double-sided village sign is at the second junction after passing the small church, known as the Bruisyard Church/Peasenhall/Cransford junction. One side of the sign, predominantly grey, shows the church, with its unusual round, slightly tapered 14th.C. tower and 13th.C. doorway, with the rest being mostly 15th.C. The church is outlined in gold. The name is across the bottom, in gold lettering.

The reverse side shows one of the Nuns of St. Clare against a nunnery window, holding a branch, possibly lime. There is an avenue of limes leading to the ancient flint church.

At the sides of the round window the letters CLA on one side and RA on the other spells Clara, the ancient form of Clare. Greenery to the right are possibly grape leaves. as Bruisyard has commercial vineyards.

Traces of the ancient college, converted in the 14th. century to the first English Nunnery of the Order of St. Clare, can be found in the grounds of an old manor, with a moat which still holds water. The metal sign has scrolled wrought-iron spandrels.

Bruisyard's tall Elizabethan hall, with 3-storied porch, was rebuilt in about 1610, on the site of a dissolved abbey of Franciscan nuns. That abbey replaced a college of 5 unsatisfactory chantry-priests, 1354-64.

DEBACH

Situated on the B1078 Needham Market to Wickham Market road, Debach was called Depebecs in the Domesday Book, meaning 'a valley or ridge by deep water'.

The village sign is dedicated to American airmen of the 493rd. Bomber Group H., killed during the second World War. It was erected in 1991 and made by U.S. engineers.

An American Flying Fortress plane is shown over the sunlit village. The galleon on the right marks the long tradition of monetary help given to local people by The Galleon Trust, founded when a portion of a galleon was presented to the village. Cornfield and sheaves denote the agricultural side of Debach, whilst the disused U.S. airfield is in the centre. The place-name is clearly shown along the bottom. The plaque on the plinth commemorates the 78th. Tactical Fighter Squadron, stationed here from April 1944 to April 1995. There was a double unveiling ceremony, with Mr. Stephen Scotcher of Debach Parish Council and Colonel David Dill, U.S.A.F. based at RAF Woodbridge officiating.

ELMSETT

Situated on the A1071, Elmsett means, from the ancient spelling of 995, Ylmesaeton, 'settlement of dwellers among the elm trees'.

The village sign is profusely decorated in filigree wrought-iron, around it and filling in the spandrels. The name is cut out in gold letters on a white background. The rest is a silhouette, showing the crown hanging from the top bar, to commemorate the Silver Jubilee of the Queen, (there is a Crown public house nearby); the church on a 'wavy hill', with an elm tree to the right on another hill. Elmsett once had elms lining the village street. The date is in the foreground, in the ridges. (It gives the impression of villagers walking down the hill (a clever touch!) in our picture, which was possibly taken from the reverse side!) The sign was made by David Oxborrow in 1977.

The village boasts a moated rectory, where John Bois once lived. He was one of the translators of the King James Bible. A tall brick silo, lovely 13th. century St. Peter's Church and beautiful views, (painted by Thomas Gainsborough in 1750) exist side by side with newer housing and business, as well as Park Wood, an ancient deer park, now of special interest to scientists. Roman remains have been found here.

BLAXHALL

In 1086, when there were 19 smallholders in the village, it was spelt in the Domesday Book as Blaccashala, meaning 'Nook of land belonging to a man called Blaec'. Blaxhall lies on the road from Snape to Tunstall on the edge of heathland near the River Alde.

The attractive village sign, in black, brown & green wrought-iron, with scroll embellishments around, is of an oval design on a sturdy wooden post, bearing the dates 1894-1994. to commemorate the village centenary.

A third-way down is the place-name. The forest is depicted in the fir trees to either side of the centre section, where two motor cycles are shown scrambling up a hill. The Woodbridge M.C.C. uses Blaxhall Pits for scrambling. Sheep denote the agricultural side of the village, when the Blaxhall Shearing Company sent teams of shearers around the farms. A room at the Ship (Sheep) Inn, now famous for continuing the tradition of singing Suffolk songs and sea shanties, was set apart before shearing time for shepherds to make appointments and pay for work done. The company is thought to go back to medieval times. Farmwork is further emphasised by the sign's top design of a horse-drawn tumbril of turf, with the farmworker adding another pitchfork full, commemorating the book 'Ask The Fellows who Cut the Hay', by local writer George Ewart Evans.

Under the 'hill', at the bottom, is stencilled the famous Blaxhall Stone, of Stone Farm, on the Wickham Market road, which is said to be growing at an alarming rate. 100 years ago it was the size of a football. Now it is said to weigh over 5 tons. Other local stones are of flint, but this one is of sandstone, an erratic or wandering stone, pushed down by the Ice Sheet when it covered the country about 150,000 years ago. Its 'parent' mass is far away at Spilsby, Lincolnshire! Flintstones 'grow' minutely as they absorb the small amounts of silica around them. Slightly acidic rainwater dissolves it to collect on flintstones to add another skin, but not sandstone. There is no scientific reason for this legend.

Blaxhall has a medieval church, with an evil face on one side of the West door and an angel's face on the other, denoting good and evil in the world; a lofty tower; 14th. C. nave and chancel; and attractive modern touches from local artist Mary Ellen Rope, buried in the churchyard in 1934. The Peace Memorial is by her, as well as 2 painted musical children in a tiny porch window. Miss Rope has work in Winchester & Salisbury Cathedrals, among other places. Dorothy Rope, another talented family member is responsible for the East window, a relief on the chancel wall and a group depicting an angel guarding Marjorie Wilson, a rector's daughter whose poems went far and wide in Arthur Mees *The Children's Newspaper*. Her grave is by the churchyard gate.

Ancestor John Roppe, churchwarden 1711, is commemorated in paint at the base of the tower beside a 12th C. carved stone.

INGHAM

The Domesday Book has the spelling as today, meaning 'Homestead or village of a man called Inga', although more recent suggestions have shown a connection with the ancient Germanic tribe, the Inguiones. On the A 134 and part of the old Culford Estate, its village sign was carved and painted by John Chelsall, with Mrs. Wilcox of Gt. Barton doing the surround.

It shows the church of St. Bartholomew, rebuilt 1861, the Old Rectory, the village inn, the Cadogan Arms and the sheltered well.

There is a marble tomb in the Church of the Holy Trinity to Beatrix Craven, Countess Cadogan, who married the 3rd. Lord Cornwallis and died in 1907. She was the daughter of Sir Stephen Fox who rebuilt the church, although the plain glass windows seem to be in 15th.C. mullions. Much of the original material was used in the tower and the nave, although the chancel appears to have been rebuilt. The vestry still has some ancient glass and there is a 13th.C. font. This large and stately church once stood at the centre of a Priory, whose ruined cloisters survive along the north aisle. In the interior can be found the base of the stone screen that once separated the parish church in the nave from the chancel end monastic church.

Two rectors have served the village for over a century: Robert Lowe, who died at 91, for 57 years and Henry Wakeham, rector in the 18th. century for 49 years.

The village boasts a massive 17th.C. barn with 11 bays.

Railway builders disturbed a Roman Graveyard, but relics from the graves are now safe in Bury St. Edmunds' Museum. The railway no longer survives either.

CULFORD

The Culford and West Stow village signs are a matching pair. They were erected by the Culford & West Stow W.I. in 1977 to celebrate the Queen's Silver Jubilee.

There are five villages: Culford, Ingham, Timworth, West Stow and Wordwell, all about 5 miles north of Bury St. Edmunds, which comprised the old Culford Estate, which operated for around 400 years, linking them culturally All are mentioned in the Domesday Book.

The Culford sign has a painting of Culford School, formerly Culford Hall, painted by pupils. Now a Methodist Residential school, the Hall was built in 1796 by the Marquis of Cornwallis. The sign's placename is at the bottom, in black lettering, in front of the school. Tree branches, top left, balance background trees to the right. The beautiful classical lines of the architecture makes the sign attractive. The first Culford Hall was built in 1591, by Sir Nicholas Bacon, stepbrother of Francis, who gave it to his son Nathanial, who is buried in the Church. His monument there is thought to have been sculptured by the unknown artist who carved the famous statue of Francis in St. Albans. In 1660 the Hall passed in marriage to the Cornwallis family, who were there for another 150 years. It went to the Cadogans in 1889, when the 5th. Earl altered it extensively. In 1935 his death duties forced the sale of the Estate. Over 50,000 acres went to the Forestry commission and The Methodist Church Education Department bought the house, for a co-educational boarding and day school for over 700 pupils. The estate included a brickworks, on the northern boundary of the Park, near West Stow, where the white bricks for the present Hall were made. The drying sheds and Kiln Cottage are still there. A footpath runs from the School to St. Mary's Church, which was rebuilt in 1856, but the Georgian flint-cased tower has been retained. Beatrix Craven, Countess Cadogan, who died in 1907, is buried in a magnificent marble tomb here.

Culford has a second church. St. Peter's at Culford Heath, now in ruins, was built to serve the more distant villagers.

WEST STOW

West Stow has a sign identical with Culford in construction. With Ingham, the village can be traced back to pre-Roman times. The Icknield Way ran from Dorset to Norfolk. It marks the northern boundary of West Stow. In the 19th.C two Romano-British cemeteries were found at Ingham. A settlement farmed there between 420 and 650 AD. Dr. Stanley West supervised the excavation of the site in 1965-72.

The West Stow sign shows a reconstruction of the Saxon village in West Stow Country Park. The sign, designed and painted by members of nearby Culford School, shows two 'halls', with vertical planks over rough walls and thatched roofs, one each side of a stream, now a canal, with sand and stones around and background trees. The placename is in bold black lettering across the sky area. The first model house was constructed in 1973 and with several more now, the site is still being expanded. The Country Park was opened as an amenity and educational resource in 1979. Black ditches of Danish/Saxon origin can be seen at a bend on the road. Both signs are in identical sturdy black frames, surrounded with wrought-iron scrolling. They also have a curved band around them, down the middle, like a crossbow.

West Stow's Church of St. Mary has been extensively restored. There is evidence of Norman craftsmen, e.g. the north doorway and some painted panels from this church can be found in the Victoria and Albert Museum in London. Sir John Crofts, Master of the Horse to Mary Tudor, built the elegant gatehouse, joined by a corridor to the Hall. Mary's shield is over the doorway. She is thought to have stayed here. Inside there are rough Elizabethan paintings on the walls, and figures reputed to be the Seven Ages of Man, from Shakespeare, each with a comment from the Cynic. These two signs make a splendid pair, one showing the estate's beginnings, the other its continuing flourishing present and future.

EARL STONHAM

The sign for this village is on the B1120 road to Stowmarket. Stonham, means 'a homestead by stone or on stony ground'. There is also Stonham Parva and Stonham Aspel (included in Suffolk Signs Book 2).

It was erected in 1977 to commemorate the Queen's Silver Jubilee. A carving of St. Mary's church surmounts the sign, with the place-name below on a white background. Beneath a centre panel shows a Roman horse-drawn chariot racing along the A140, the old Roman Road. A Roman settlement was here and the fine 13th.C church is a masterpiece of fine carving, especially the roof. It has medieval wall paintings and unique hourglasses.

This village is in a traditional farming area and local trades are depicted in the wings and brackets of the sign. To the left of the chariot the blacksmith can be seen at work, with the farmer to the right. On the solid spandrels to the left a woman is shown at the ancient village pump, with basket-making shown on the right. The top of the post holds the date plaque, ER II 1977.

This attractive and colourful sign was carved by Harry Carter of Swaffham and stands on one of the village greens. The village is scattered around 3 ancient Greens, Forward Green, Middlewood Green and Broad Green.

Until 1988, when he died, Mr. Bob Haggar had been the village blacksmith for 80 years, breaking all records.

FAKENHAM MAGNA

Situated south of Thetford on the B1088 road, Fakenham Magna, is spelt in the Domesday Book as 'Litla Fachenham', 'homestead of a man called Facca'. The attractive sign, made by Brian Gaze, has a plaque which reads 'BG designs 0359-30204. It is oval in an attractive wrought-iron frame with scroll embellishments.

The sign shows the grey-towered, red-roofed church, which has an Elizabethan bell. In the centre is the green-painted village pump with wildfowl to the right foreground and the stream spanned by an attractive arched bridge. The place-name in green lettering to match most of the sign, on a white 'ribbon' background forms the bottom of the oval. A duck is on the stream and the yellow irises to the right balance the yellow and white wild flowers to the left above the ends of the placename. The background trees show that here we find some of Suffolk's finest woodland.

Opposite the church is the thatched cottage where poet Robert Bloomfield visited his mother, who was born there. He immortalised in verse the ghost story of the lady crossing Euston Park, terrified by heavy footsteps following her. Reaching her home she fainted and came round not to confront a beastly human, but a young donkey which had strayed from its mother.

The church is very old, with traces of Saxon work in the chancel. It has 2 small Norman windows in the mainly 13th. & 14th. century walls, a door with extra long hinges and an evil-looking doorknocker, an ancient stoup in the porch, a piscena and 15th. C. screen which has been restored and an early font. There are quoins (corner stones) at each end of the nave.

Today the village is largely occupied by Honington Airfield.

The white-bricked Georgian Rushford Hall, beside the Little Ouse, has beautiful wrought-iron gates. Elizabethan chimney stacks can be found at Field Farm.

(N.B. It is listed as 'Little Fakenham' on most maps.)

CRATFIELD

Situated 6 miles west of Halesworth, Cratfield was spelt as Cratafelda in the Domesday Survey, 'open land of a man called Craeta.' Its parish records date back to 1490 and show that 'church ales' were cheerfully drunk on certain feast days. On October 10th. 1553 expences are listed for one soldier to help guard Princess Mary at Framlingham.

Its carved wooden sign, badly in need of weatherproofing when we photographed it, shows its four Greens: Bell Green, Swan Green, North Green and Silverleys, meaning region of trees.

The sign, carved by Mrs. Davies of Corpusty, is solid, with a capped top. Underneath are leaves (for Silverleys), a bell to the right and swan to the left. At the bottom, a peacock-shaped top half of a compass dial showing an N at the top depicts North Green. (Maybe peacocks once roamed on North Green.) It was erected to commemorate Elizabeth II, as E2R is carved below between the spandrels. It stands just inside the country garden of the old school, now a private dwelling, opposite Walpole Road on the B1123, Halesworth to Harleston road.

The church has a fine medieval font, which was damaged but not destroyed by Cromwell. There are 20 clerestory windows over 500 years old. Though restored in the 15th. C., much of the original remains, with fragments of a screen and a clock bell in an oak frame, dated c1400, donated by William Aleys. Town House, the original Guildhall of St. Edmund, adjoins the churchyard.

COTTON

Cotton boasts a most unusual village sign, made by Mr. Stewart of Finningham Road. It depicts the monk, Bartholomew, an early East Anglian historian born at Cotton Hall. Behind him is a moat in the form of a letter 'C', as Cotton is reputed to have more moats than any other Suffolk village. The sign was erected in 1977 to commemorate the Silver Jubilee of Queen Elizabeth II.

Cotton's St. Andrew's church is a gem. Built in the 14th.C and added to in the 15th., it is larger than expected for this village, but with its double hammerbeam roof, rich carvings, medieval glass, exquisite Jacobean pulpit and beautifully decorated porch, it is well-worth a visit.

EASTON

Easton is situated north of the A12, south of Framlingham. It is named in the Domesday book as Estuna, meaning east farmstead or village. Its village sign was presented by the Easton and Letheringsett W.I. in 1969. It depicts the longest ribbon, or Serpentine wall in the world, enclosing Easton Park Estate, home to the Earls of Rochester and Dukes of Hamilton. The wall and house were built by Anthony Wingfield in 1607, later created a baronet. The present 19th.C house is mainly Edwardian.

The placename is in gold lettering across the wall, with a painted silhouette of a huntsman and his hounds on the turf below, denoting the Easton Harriers. The sign is framed in black-wrought iron and sits on scrolled spandels.

The beautiful 14th.C. church contains monuments to the Wingfields and Rochfords and has two Elizabethan Wingfield family pews, complete with canopies! The tower has a square bottom and octagonal top.

Today Easton is more well-known for its Agricultural College and Farm park, but it still boasts some lovely old houses....and the wall.

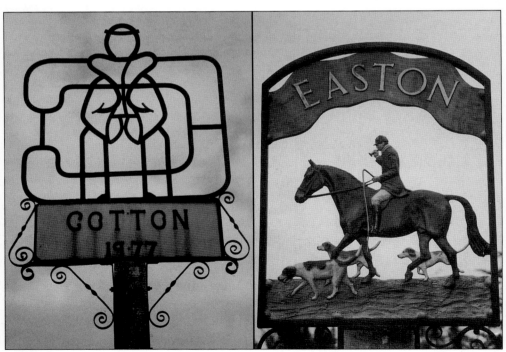

ERWARTON

Situated at the tip of the Shotley peninsula, where the River Stour and the Orwell meet, near the B1456 road, the Domesday Book records this village as Eurewardestuna, 'farmstead of a man called Eoforweard' (Olde English). Situated opposite the church, its sign, made in Hadleigh from a design by Mr. Robert Gibson-Jarvis of Erwarton, must be one of the highest in Suffolk.

It depicts the crown of Queen Anne (Boleyn) and coat of arms of the Calthorpe family, the unusual Jacobean gateway of the Hall, flags of Anne and Henry VIII and the placename over the gateway in warm peach. The sign is a silhouette in a black wrought-iron frame.

A row of village houses, Boleyn Place, recalls the legend that the heart of Anne Boleyn was buried in the church here. Anne's aunt married a Calthorpe of Calthorpe Hall and Anne spent part of her childhood here. It is said that Henry VIII visited her by yacht. When she met her unhappy death, friends are said to have taken her heart to bury in the church which she loved. During extensive renovations in 1837, a heart-shaped casket was found containing a handful of dust. The story was honoured and the casket reburied in a vault beneath the organ. The church is 14th. century, with the said renovations. There is a monument to Isabel Davillers, daughter of the earliest known lords of the manor. A wealthy heiress, she married Sir Robert Bacon.

During the Civil War stern loyalists fought until their ammunition ran out, then took down the church bells and used the metal to continue to battle against the Roundheads. A tiny village with a monumental history and a high sign!

DRINKSTONE

Drinkstone was spelt Drincestune in 1050 'the farmstead of a man called Drenic'. South of the A45, east of Bury St. Edmunds, its sign is on Drinkstone Green. It was designed and carved by local craftsman Henry John Gibbs and erected in 1977 for the Queen's Silver Jubilee. It is an unusual lychgate

LONG MELFORD

Long Melford is probably known to most television viewers as the place where the *Lovejoy* serial was filmed. Famous for its High Street with a proliferation of antique shops, it has a beautiful double-sided sign depicting the life of its residents in medieval times. This is in keeping with its fine timber-framed 16th. century buildings. Opposite the sign, which is set on a green, is the Bull Inn, a wonderful example of Elizabethan architecture, now a Hotel. In 1648 a murder was committed there, when a Roundhead slew a Cavalier.

Long Melford's name in Roman times is unknown, but the straight main street is possibly a Roman road, no doubt giving the name 'Long'. Melford comes from the mill ford in the centre, which now is crossed by a bridge. The magnificent church of High Trinity has been called the most beautiful in Suffolk and is at the opposite end of the Green. Sir William Cordell, a Speaker of the House of Commons welcomed Queen Elizabeth I to Melford Hall during her Royal Progress through Suffolk. His impressive tomb is in the church chancel. 15th. century, the Church is a wool church, 250 foot long, built by the affluence of the medieval woollen industry. Its Tower, restored in Victorian times, is 180 foot high.

Another moated Tudor hall, with fine grounds, Kentwell, was the home of the Clopton family, mainly responsible for rebuilding the church as it is today. There is a small chapel called the Clopton Chantry.

The sign was erected in 1978 in memory of C.R. (Dick) Kingston, who was chairman of the Parish Council, in recognition of his service between 1954 and 1976.

The colourful carved wooden sign records two features of past village life. On one side the main panel depicts workers at a loom, commemorating the association with the flourishing wool trade. On the reverse side is the Old Horse Fair, with horses and traders, held on the Green for centuries, but now merely an entertainment fair.

Below the village name, on both sides of the sign, the 'Long Melford', a famous local long purse, no doubt manufactured to hold the gold accrued from the wool trade, can be seen, along with a group of elm trees, formerly on the Green but now gone, recently having succumbed to Dutch elm desease.

The two red shields, are interesting in that the one facing the Elizabethan moated Melford Hall is inscribed ER I, while the one looking over the village has ER II on it.

The attractive sign was made by Harry Carter of Swaffham.

There were formerly three corn mills in Long Melford, six malt houses, a foundry, two milliners, a tinsmith, a rope manufacturer and a whitesmith, which will give some idea of the size of this village when it was actually a small West Suffolk Town, with silk weaving one of its main industries well into the last century.

(Pictures Centre Pages)

DRINKSTONE

(Continued):shape, to depict the 14th.C church. In the 'gateway', Drinkstone Mill, built in 1689 and still working, is shown, plus a medieval tile that can be found below the lectern in the church. The post has ER II 1977 written down it. Round carved spandrels, possibly denoting more medieval artifacts, complete the unusual design.

The church contains beautiful remains of a 15th.C. screen, ancient glass and a richly carved chest. A strange legend persists, that when Joshua Grigby III. died at Drinkstone Park, he was buried by his own request in a corner of his garden. The land was hallowed and in 1829 he was buried beneath a mulberry tree, sitting up, above ground, with his tomb built around him. This was his widow's doing, to spite his mistress, to whom he had said, "You shall not have a penny of my money until I am lying under the ground"!

OFFTON

Spelt in the Domesday Book as Offetuna, 'farmstead of a man called Offa' (Old English name), the village of Offten lies N.W. of Ipswich.

The attractive sign depicts Offa, legendary King of Mercia and bravest of Byrhtnoth's men at the battle of Maldon in 991. He is painted in an oval frame which doubles as the 'O' of the place-name.

The fortified building depicted in the other panel is the Castle of William of Ambli, who lived during the reign of Stephen. The castle commanded the highest point, as was necessary and while there are no tangible remains, the mound and moat is meticulously preserved.

Nearby St. Mary's Church was desecrated by the Puritan William Dowsing. Mainly 14th.C., there are later additions. The tower has eight bells and dedicated bellringers down the centuries have worked hard for these, the oldest being early 1500s and the latest dedicated in 1983.

OTLEY

Otley was spelled Otelega in the Domesday Book, meaning 'woodland clearing of a man called Otta', or 'Place of Oaks'. It is on the B1079 road north of Ipswich. The village sign was erected to commemorate the 60th. Anniversary of the W.I. in 1979. It was commissioned from Mr. E. Londbottom of Otley to be carved as a wood collage on a dark background, in a solid wooden frame. The Gosnold Shield is in the top centre, with the name scrolled below. Under that, to the left a sheaf of wheat denotes the first inhabitant of Otley Hall who took the first wheat grain to the U.S.A. On the right is the sailing ship of Bartholomew Gosnold, who discovered Cape Cod and set up Jamestown in Virginia in the early 17th.C. Beneath that the placename is carved in large white letters. Oak leaves, white Tudor roses and grapes (to depict the local vineyards) surround the whole collage, tributes to both Otley, England and America. One of the oldest serving Rectors, Samuel Rogers, laboured here for 67 years in the 18th. century. Today Otley is more noted for its Agricultural experimental and educational Centre. Otley's 13th.C. St. Mary's church has many gems, but in 1950, when the floor of the vestry was raised, a baptistry font was discovered, 6 feet long, 2 feet eight inches deep and always full, the water level maintaining itself naturally. Otley's Baptist chapel was built around 1800, so the font obviously pre-dates that.

HEPWORTH

Hepworth is spelt as Hepworda in the Domesday Book, meaning, 'enclosure of a man called Heppa' and lies off the A143 Bury St. Edmunds to Diss road, but it was occupied much earlier. In stone pits near the church a hand axe was found and dated at 300,000B.C. also three axe heads from 7,000B.C. one dug out in a new grave in the church-yard.

The beautifully carved village sign with 3D effect manufactured by Mr. Allen, was designed and painted by Mr. Leigh. It was erected by the village for the Silver Jubilee of Queen Elizabeth II in 1977 and a crown is set into the post. It shows St. Peter's Church with its red roof tiles, surrounded by trees. It was thatched until a disastrous fire in 1898, when fortunately the treasured 14th. C. wooden font cover, over 12 foot high, and massive church door were saved. There is a fine hammerbeam roof and paved black and white marble blocks in the chancel. The agricultural nature of the village is shown in the horse and tumbril of hay, field of sheaves and wild flowers and hips above the place-name. The hips have a special village significance.

A weekly market was held in Hepworth, when the village boasted 3 forges, a mill, 3 inns, 3 public charities and 4 shops.

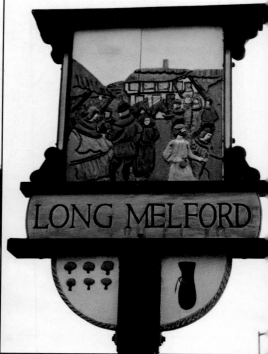

PALGRAVE

PETTAUGH

PALGRAVE

Palgrave lies on the A143 road south of Diss. Its name was spelt the same as early as 962 and means 'grove where poles are found'. The sign, opposite St. Peter's church, was erected by parishioners' public subscriptions in memory of George E. Clarke and Robert B. Rolfe in 1985, to commemorate their hard work for the community. It was designed by Tony Lees, carved by Mr. Goater, a woodcarver and restorer of musical instruments, and painted by his wife.

Emblems of trades are carved down the post of the sign: wheat, a weavers' mark and a shepherd's crook. Sturdily constructed, with a solid place-name base, a carved blacksmith works at his anvil, reinforcing the theme of old village crafts. The sign stands on a solid brick and cobblestone plinth.

Palgrave has some fine plastered and thatched cottages. A 1787 headstone in the churchyard shows a waggoner and wagon, drawn by 6 horses, still clearly visible due to the skilled engraving.

Thomas Martin, F.A.S. (1697-1771 is commemorated in the flushwork of the church porch. He collected ancient documents and impoverished himself in older age by spending all he had on antiquities. George Crabb came from Palgrave and from 1774-85 eminent classical writer Anne Letitia Barbauld helped her husband in a boarding school for boys in the village. It produced such distinguished scholars as Chief Justice Lord Denham, antiquarian Sir William Gill and Walter Taylor, who 'made Walter Scott a poet, inspired by his ballad, Lenore'. It was for the boys in the school that Mrs. Barbauld wrote, *Hymns in Prose for Children,* her best work.

PETTAUGH

The colourful village sign at Pettaugh stands on the busy crossroads at the junction of the old Debenham to Ipswich turnpike, which is crossed by the A1120 Stowmarket to Yoxford road. The population of about 130 was the same when the Domesday Book spelt its name as Petehaga, 'enclosure of a man called Peohtred'. (Olde English name)

The village sign, erected in 1997, stands on the corner at the crossroads. The sign features the tall post mill which stood at this junction with the two-horse drawn plough and farmer below. Trees and furrows complete that part of the picture. A bright yellow band below has a centre section with a painting of the church of St. Catherine, which was served at one time by the monks from Leiston Abbey. They would have made the journey on foot. On either side panel is depicted, on the right, an anvil, remembering the part the blacksmith of old played in village commerce, and to the left a heavily bound book. Finding no references to a library here, one can only assume it shows the connection with William Shakespeare and Sir John Falstolf (Falstaff), whose family owned Pettaugh Hall around 1524 - 1670. Beneath this is the place-name, in black lettering on the same bright yellow, above a sturdy post.

The village also had its own shoemaker and wheelwright. All the old crafts have now gone, but the village spirit remains, hence the success in erecting a village sign.

The 14th.C. church and tower, with a 15th.C. top has an old priest's door, a 500 year-old font, a 16th.C. brass of one of the Falstolf family, a reading desk, dated 1615, with strangely carved poppyheads and its original chancel.

MILDENHALL

Mildenhall, a small market town on the River Lark, 12 miles west of Bury St. Edmunds, was spelt as Mildenehale around 1050, but Mitdenehala in the Domesday book, meaning 'middle nook of land' or possibly 'Nook of land of a man called Mildha'. Its sturdy wooden sign is in the form of a quartered shield with the crossbars in red. Cut out each side of the black lettered nameplate at the ends of the horizontal bar are stencils of a hammer and an arrowhead. Six coats of arms are painted down the vertical bar. An extremely full sign, the plain background ensures that it never appears too much. The top left quarter shows its ancient medieval wooden Market Cross with its fine lead roof resting on rough-hewn pillars. To the right is the Church with white cloud above and tree to the left.

The bottom left quarter depicts the ancient port, now closed to navigation, with the old mill across the river, with its lock pen, and the fish completing the picture. Daniel Defoe refers to coal, corn and iron carried by barge here in 1722. Navigation continued up to Bury St. Edmunds in medieval times. To the right is countryside with a plane flying above. Mildenhall is now more well known for the airbase there, but its aviation fame started in 1934 when it became international news. The Air Race to Australia started from Mildenhall, when Charles Scott and Campbell Black reached Melbourne in just 71 hours, the fastest journey across earth ever known up to then.

Stone Age man was here, with the arrowhead to commemorate it. There are Saxon Graves at Warren Hill.

In 1042 the manor was given to Bury Abbey, 'that the monks might eat wheaten and not barley-bread'. It is believed that the collector of tithes, Cellarius lived on or near the site of the present house named the Priory in the S.W. corner of the churchyard. A play entitled 'St. Thomas' was performed in the north churchyard in 1505. It is easy to see why so many coats of arms are featured, since many can be found in the Church, Sir Henry North (1556-1620) built a manor house on the north side of the church. The south aisle contains his altar tomb. His grandson, Thomas Hanmer lies in the chancel. A baronet and M.P. at 24, he became Speaker at 37, defended the Protestant succession and retired when that was secured, to produce the first printed works of Shakespeare, correcting errors in the text. It was discovered in 1917, called the Hanmer Fourth Folio and now resides in the Bodleian library. William Bunbury, Vicar of Mildenhall succeeded to the manor in 1747 and it remained in the family until 1933, when the house was demolished and the bricks used to build bungalows in Church Walk. The church is 13th. C. as well as the old mill. Originally called St. Andrew's, the church was dedicated to St. Mary in 1895. It is 170 foot long, with its tower 120 foot high, topped with a bright weathercock. The piscena and sedilia were there when Magna Carta was signed and the fine hammerbeam roof on a par with the rest of the fine woodcarving. Sir Henry de Barton is buried here. Lord Mayor of London after Agincourt, he instigated street lighting by asking residents to hang a lighted lantern outside each house after dark.

Mildenhall's greatest treasure is in the British Museum, the fantastically preserved collection of late Roman silver dishes, ploughed up during the Second World War and known as the Mildenhall Treasure. The sign stands on an attractive stone plinth with seven steps up to the post.

(Picture Centre Pages)

SHOTTISHAM

On the B1083 from Woodbridge, this village was listed as Scotesham in the Domesday Book, meaning 'a homestead of a man called Scot.'

Its beautiful sign, in pastel shades on a mid-blue background, is in a black wrought-iron frame with scrolling above and below. A wreath of corn stalks and daisies frame a picture of the church tower peeping out through trees, with the old mill in front, beside the winding river.

It was painted by Mrs. Jean Clarke, R.W.S., who lives in the village, and manufactured by MCR Engineering of Woodbridge.

The present water mill, now converted to residential use, is believed to be on the same site as the old mill, mentioned in the Domesday Book as being in the Manor of Wood Hall. The mill was working up to the 1950s, with an associated coal merchant trading for some years after that.

The Church of St. Margaret towers over the village, visible for miles, with clusters of cottages forming attractive views. Just below the church, the thatched Sorrel Horse Inn dates back in parts to the 16th. and 17th centuries.

Flint arrowheads and pottery finds go back to Roman times and in the light sandy soil it is still possible to find an occasional fossilised shark's tooth or shell.

William Kett was the vicar here for 50 years.

THORPENESS

Thorpeness, about two miles along the coast road from Aldeburgh, was originally a hamlet of Aldringham called Thorpe, which later became larger than its parent in Tudor times. At the beginning of the 20th century its prosperity centred around approximately 25 fishing smacks. The timber Thorpe Fisherman's Bethel Hall, built in 1890, probably afforded the entire social as well as spiritual needs of the population, but with a flash of inspiration, this insignificant little place was transformed into a popular leisure centre.

The sign was donated by Thorpeness Golf Club for the Thorpeness Resident's Association in 1990. It is situated on the corner, in front of the boathouse and entrance to the local Meare, and shows its old postmill, removed from Aldringham with the intention that it would pump water into an enormous tank. The tank is the other feature of the sign, standing around 80 feet high and known as 'The House in the Clouds'. The 'house' is actually a camouflage of the converted tank, while underneath is the real house, occupied by a family. The whole edifice has the appearance of a multi-storied fairy-tale design.

Visitors are pleasantly surprised to see the little house, across the fields or behind the Meare, high up into the sky. It is all part of the imaginative village conversion, carried out from 1910-1930, and planned by Stuart Ogilvie, with the assistance of designers W.G.Wilson and F.Forbes Glennie. The magnificent centrepiece of the plan was the 60-acre Meare created out of the marshes, now a popular boating lake. The postmill, which was built at Aldringham in 1803 and moved to Thorpeness in 1923, was restored in 1978 and now serves as a heritage information centre. Thorpeness still retains a fishing village image, with its weather-boarded houses, but from early this century it has been a purpose-built 'model' village.

(Pictures Centre Pages)

31

GREAT BARTON

From the Old English Beretun, 'a barley farm, grange where wheat is stored', Great Barton is 2½ miles N.E. of Bury St. Edmunds. The sign stands prominently on the A143, erected in 1977 for the Queen's Silver Jubilee.
Its sign, carved by Harry Carter of Swaffham, shows 'Bertuna the Gleaner' taken from the famous painting, 'The Gleaner'. The woman is bent double beneath her load, still picking up more. Wheat stalks on the brown wooden spandrels complete the theme. The place-name is between, with black lettering on a white background.
The village is well-scattered over an area larger than its great neighbour. It was a Saxon settlement, becoming the granary for the abbey of Bury St. Edmunds. Icepits Woods have huge excavations, confirming that it was the abbey's ice store. Sir Charles Bunbury of Barton Hall owned the first two Derby winners. A village legend has it that the first one, Diomed, can be seen in the park of the Old Barton Hall, destroyed by fire in 1914, on the eve of Derby Day in spectral form. The Bunbury family built almshouses and the village school, with a public house 2 miles from the village, so that churchgoers would not be tempted on the way to and from church! The church of the Holy Innocents was surrounded by houses, until the plague, when people moved away from the source of the infection. During the Civil War, every angel in the old hammerbeam roof lost its head, except one. The soldier lost his footing and fell on the flagstones to his death. Retribution indeed!

GRUNDISBURGH

The Domesday Book listed the village as Grundesburch, 'stronghold near the foundation of a building'. 'The unusual sign at Grundisburgh resembles a gate, complete with top central spikes, with a centre panel inset depicting the Garter Banner of the 2nd. Baron Cranworth, three golden leopards' heads on a black background. Grundisburgh Hall and estate were bought from the Blois estate in 1770 by the Gurdons. In 1899 Robert Gurdon, M.P. became a peer and chose the name Cranworth from a Norfolk village where he had lived. His silk banner now hangs in the church, brought from the Garter stall in Windsor Chapel.
Thomas A'Wall, of the Salters' Company, extended his father's home, Basts, in the 15th. century and financed the Lady chapel, built at St. Mary's Church.
Weekly markets and annual fairs used to be held on the Green, where the River Finn runs under little bridges. Basket-making was also a successful village trade.
The sign, created by local skill and effort, was unveiled 21st. October 1992 by Miss Vera Gadd.

HARLESTON

In the Domesday Book it was spelt as Herolnestuna, 'farmstead of a man named Heoruwulf'. Its sign, erected to celebrate the Silver Jubilee of Queen Elizabeth II., is on Harleston Road near the village green. The wooden shield was carved by Mr. R. Turner, and the decorated wrought-iron work by students of the local High School. It depicts leaves from nearby lime trees, which form an avenue across the village green, in the shield-shaped panel, set into a square wrought-iron frame, embellished with scrolling around and under it. Under the leaves there is a banner reading : 1952 JUBILEE 1977. Various blue dots on either side each represents 10 residents, therefore the 5 dots on the left, above the '1952' reveals that there were 50 residents then, whereas the 15 dots on the right, above 1977, shows that the population trebled in the first 25 years of the Monarch's reign.

It was designed by Mr. Brian Wright, who thought the village was always known as Harleston Green. There is no evidence of this in the church registers. However it would cause less confusion with Norfolk's Harleston, only 25 miles away!

Over a century ago the village was united with Onehouse, with the church room there used for functions. Harleston Green was actually a piece of swamp land. During World War I Mr. Terry of Harleston Hall drained it, giving better grazing for the domestic animals. Many new herbs were introduced, which a doctor from Haughley regularly collected for medicinal purposes. The thatched church only consists of a nave, with no tower. It was formerly perhaps just a chapel for the Hall. It has medieval features and a pre-Norman dedication to Augustine. The Green has 16th.C cottages. Stow Lodge, originally the workhouse, cost £12,000 to build in 1781, more 'a gentleman's seat than a receptacle for paupers'. There is a pauper's graveyard.

Harleston, off the A45 N.W. of Stowmarket, has also received the Best Kept Village Award.

MENDLESHAM

The Domesday Book spells this as Mundlesham, 'homestead of a man called Myndel'. The village is west of the A140 and south of Diss. The attractive village sign, carved by Harry Carter of Swaffham, was presented to the parish by the W.I. to commemorate their 50th. Anniversary, 1926-1976.

The sign is double-sided. In the form of a shield in front of crossed swords, one side, with a red background, depicts Sir John Knivet, knight in armour, whose brass, 1417, is in St. Mary's Church. The Knivets were lords of the manor in the 15th. C.

The reverse side, with a pale blue background, has two vertical panels. One shows the famous Mendlesham Chair, manufactured by Dan Day from 1780 - 1820. His son was reputed to have worked for Sheraton. The other side features the group of Mendlesham Martyrs, burned at the stake during the reign of Queen Mary I.

The place-name is under the shield, with black lettering on a white background, above green-painted wooden spandrels.

In the 1851 census 1500 people lived here, mainly supported by weaving. A weaver's window in Front Street and a retting pit in a nearby field bears witness to this.

The beautiful church of St. Mary has 13th., 14th. & 15th.C. features, with a magnificent tall font cover, made in 1630 by John Turner and 2 Dan Dare unique Chairs, traditionally made with yew and fruitwood, with an elm seat. The Priest's Chamber holds a collection of rare medieval and Tudor armour, an Elizabethan long-bow and 2 standard pewter jugs designed to check correct measures in local hostelries. There was a wartime airbase here, the buildings now used as industrial warehouses. The 1,000 foot T.V. mast is a local landmark. A Market Charter was granted in 1281 and there is an ancient Preaching Stone, used by itinerant preachers, especially in John Wesley's day.

The poet and weather prophet Thwaite-Orlando Whistlecraft was born here in 1810 and died in 1893.

MENDLESHAM GREEN

The simple village sign at Mendlesham Green, a satellite 1½ miles south of the main village, holds the place-name in black lettering on a white background, surrounded by filigree wrought-iron scrolling. It is topped by a wrought-iron wheel to commemorate the Arbon family, wheelwrights in the village for many years. The sign was made by Mr. N.K. Steward of Cotton for the W.I.s Golden Jubilee in 1978.

It stands in front of the field containing the Armada beacon with its hanging sign recording the 300th. anniversary of the defeat of the Armada fleet, with the dates 1588 - 1988. The place-name here is arranged around it's shield-shaped bottom.

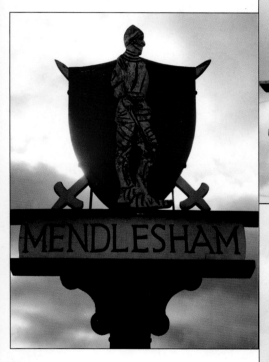

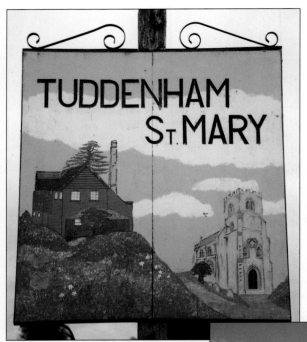

TUDDENHAM ST. MARY

Spelt as Todenham in the Domesday Book, meaning 'village of a man called Tudda', Tuddenham St. Mary is east of the All and south of Mildenhall. Its sign depicts two fine buildings, the redundant water mill, which stood by the River Linnett, a small tributary of the Lark, and the fine 14th.C. church of St. Mary, which was restored in Victorian times. The sign is complemented by wild flowers because the village is noted for several species, such as fingered speedwell and the rupture wort.

The W.I. erected the sign in 1977 to commemorate the Silver Jubilee of Queen Elizabeth II. Situated on a wide green, it was made by Mr. Shafto. The date is written down the post.

There has been a mill here since Saxon times, mentioned in the Domesday book, but the present one dates from the 18th.C. and has been renovated and converted into a successful restaurant, with exposed beams and featuring the water wheel. The river was used to carry flint and grain in barges during the 19th.C.

The village has a RAF station, with U.S. bases nearby at Lakenheath and Mildenhall. and Tuddenham Fen is well-known to nature lovers. Many of the buildings were of flint: the old Bakery, Smithy and original Methodist Church, which was bombed in World War II and rebuilt in 1951.

One of the church bells is dated 1591 and there are registers from 1563. The legendary Temple Bridge is reputed to be a hold-up point used by highwaymen, on the old coaching route through the village.

TUDDENHAM ST. MARTIN

St. Martin, the name of the village church, prefixes Tuddenham, meaning 'homestead of a man called Tudda', in this village, 4 miles N.E. of Ipswich. The village sign, erected in 1996, is situated at the approach of the bridge on the main road through the village. Attractively silhouetted in a black wrought-iron frame, the design is colourful and attractive. The frame holds a centre plate showing Michael Wolversten, who lost his estates and almost his life in the Civil War, after fighting loyally for the king and having to witness his execution. St. Martin's Church is featured below that, with a brick-maker in the foreground, with the brickworks which gave employment to residents in the past. The clay was dug at the top of the village and washed in a pit behind Oak House, then sent through a large pipe behind the Street cottages to the brickyard near the present Brickfield House.

The place-name, in bright red lettering on a white background, completes the design. The whole is on a sturdy post. Double-sided, the picture is shown in reverse on the other side.

Contemporary with the brickmaking, was a forge and a windmill. A later mill produced animal feeds and malt and supported a score of families. It was closed in 1982 by owner Douglas Green.

There is a 14th.C. fountain near the River Fynn, providing refreshment for drovers en route to Ipswich. The church has a 15th.C. west tower, Norman doorway and font said to be the oldest in the country, complete with tall carved cover. The chancel screen was installed and dedicated after World War II. It was made from Suffolk oak from the windmills at Ashfield and Earl Soham. There is a memorial to Michael Wolversten and the East window tells the story of the rector's son, a young midshipman, who lost his life climbing a mast whilst trying to secure a sail to the mast in a hurricane.

IXWORTH

In around 1025, this village name was spelt Gyxeweorde, changing to Giswortha in the Domesday book, meaning 'enclosure of a man called Gicsa'. Ixworth, a village close to the Icknield Way, was used by Iceni settlers. The Romans later developed this road and built the Peddars Way, which runs from Colchester through Ixworth, to Holme-next-the Sea in Norfolk. Associated thus with travellers all through its history, the village is now bypassed on the A143 road to Bury St. Edmunds. Its beautiful and colourful sign depicts this, with early foot and horse traffic. Designed by Brian Gaze and erected in 1983, it shows three pack horses with a man leading them, against a background of hedge and tree. The tree shape forms the top of the sign. The green, depicting the country life of the village is repeated in the green name lettering under the design, written boldly on a white background. The whole is set on a solid post and oval shaped supports, to complete the shape of the sign. The village boasts remains of Roman building, probably part of a settlement near the Iceni camp. Ixworth Abbey, built on the site of an Augustine 12th. century Priory, is on this same site.

In the dissolution, Henry VIII built Nonsuch Palace for Anne Boleyn. To obtain the site, he displaced the Coddington family, who owned it. In return, he gave them Ixworth, which he had stolen from the Church Establishment.

In the church of St. Mary are tombs of Richard Coddington and his wife. An inscription above records the gift from the King. St. Mary's is richly decorated with flint flushwork. Mainly 14th. century, there are additions from the 15th. 16th. and 19th. It stands near the High Street.

Ixworth is rich in old buildings from all periods, many of them timber-framed. The oldest is late 14th. century.

The village prospered in the 18th. and early 19th. centuries, with over a thousand population and daily coaches to London, Bury St. Edmunds and Norwich, better than the service today! It declined steadily, until after World War II, when new building led to an increasing population once more, with now around 2,500 residents. With severe traffic problems, the bypass, planned from the 1920s, materialised in 1986.

UFFORD

Ufford lies off the A12, south of Wickham Market. It is easy to miss its sign, because the village once consisted of an Upper and a Lower street, about half a mile apart. Missing it would be a pity, as it also serves as the directional signpost. It can be found by turning off the 'main' road through Crownfields. Designed by John Reid, a former resident, it was commissioned by the W.I. and made by Hector Moore of Brandeston Forge. Mary Moore did the patternwork and artwork.

A Suffolk Punch stallion stands proudly in the top arch to commemorate Sam Crisp's famous horse of Ufford, foaled in 1768, which founded the famous breed. It was advertised, at a five shilling fee for service, as a 'five-year-old bright stallion, standing a full 15½ hands'. Never named, he was 'horse 404'.

Ufford derives its name from Wuffa's ford, referring to the 6th. century King of the East Angles whose palace was nearby. The stylised crown and waves in the bottom half of the sign, beneath the place-name, are symbolic of this. Uffa founded the Uffinga Dynasty. The crown of King Redwold was found in 1687 in Rendlesham Forest.

After the Norman Conquest the Peyton family from the Hall at Ramsholt settled here and took the name of Ufford. Robert de Ufford whose son was created a baron in 1337, was Chief Justice of Ireland in 1269.

Ufford's 12th century church is said to have the most beautiful font cover in the country, probably in the world. Villagers defended it with their lives from Dowsing's iconoclasts, hence its survival. Spiralling up to an 18 foot cone, it is of intricate and delicate craftmanship, a worthy memorial to those skills of over 500 years ago.

The two inns, the Crown and the White Lyon, date from the 17th. century as do the almshouses near the church. There were also Sickhouses, built to provide isolation for the infected during the Plague. Outside the church, redundant today but still in good condition, are 18th. century stocks and a whipping post.

The Rev.Richard Lovekin, Rector from 1621 -1678 died at 110 years old, still taking services and performing his pastoral duties up to the Sunday before his demise.

NEEDHAM MARKET

Called Nedham in the 13th.C., then Nedeham Market in 1511, Anglo Saxon for 'A Home in Need', Needham Market was granted its market charter by Henry III. The market and local trade flourished until the plague in 1665. There has never been a market there since, although the right to hold it still exists.

The village tried in vain to contain the plague, putting chains across streets to stop people spreading the deadly infection. Chain Bridge, to the west and Chain House Farm to the east still remind us of this. The 'Sick houses' still exist in Crown Street where those who did not die were nursed. Food was exchanged and the money used sterilised before being passed on. Victims were buried in a mass grave outside the village, now the site of a housing estate.

The village sign was erected in 1951 to commemorate the Festival of Britain. It is sturdily constructed of wood, with greyhounds either side supporting the coat of Arms of the Ashburton family painted on a pale blue background by local resident Mrs. Moore. One of the first private banks in the country was opened here in 1744 when the town was thriving.

The church of St. John the Baptist is in the High Street. Its medieval roof is widely acknowledged to be the most ambitious and brilliant carpentry project in England. The beauty and craftmanship of the huge hammerbeam roof, as high again as the bottom half of the church, is incredible. This quaint church has a clock tower on its porch and is rich in carving.

The 300 year old Congregational church had as a minister Joseph Priestley, who 'discovered' oxygen. Robert Uvedale, the botanist, brought cedars from Lebanon here. One still flourishes at the Bank House. The village, once a thriving town, is expanding again but lovely old medieval houses and features like the huge split oak and an arch with an 18' span, in The Ancient House, point to the rich historical importance of this place, market or no.

REDLINGFIELD

Redlingfield's attractive sign was erected for the Silver Jubilee of Queen Elizabeth II in 1977, in memory of James Risk. It was carved in cedarwood by Harry Carter of Swaffham.

The village was listed in the Domesday Book as Radinghafelda, meaning 'open land of a man called Raedel or Raedia'. The village lies S.E. of Diss, between the B1077 and B1118 roads.

The sign is surmounted by a model of the Benedictine Nunnery, built in 1120, on the site of the present church. Its dormitory is still used as a barn in a nearby farmyard. In 1427 one of its Prioresses, Isobel Hermyte, modelled in three dimension on the sign, owned up to not going to confession or mass and to have succumbed to the charms of a bailiff. She resigned but the whole convent was made to fast on bread and beer each Friday!

St. Andrew's Church is depicted on the full width of the sign, showing the truncated gable-roofed tower and the red-brick chancel with a stone-built nave between. There are stocks in the foreground, which are now preserved in the church tower.

An eagle is depicted on the stem and attractive plinth, denoting Roman occupation.

NEEDHAM MARKET

LE ROY ET L'ESTAT

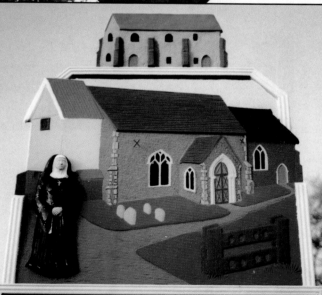

REDLINGFIELD

REDGRAVE

Redgrave lies on the B1113 off the A143 Bury St. Edmunds to Diss road. Spelt as Redgrafe in the 11th.C., meaning 'a reedy pit or red grove' it has a long history, with Redgrave Hall Estate naturally providing most of the village employment in past days. Ulfketel, Earl of the East Angles, who was killed in 1016 in a battle with the Danes, first gave the Lordship of Redgrave to the abbey of Bury. After the Dissolution of the Monasteries, Henry VIII gave the manor to Thomas Darcy, from whom it passed to the Bacon family. The Hall was built in 1211 by Sampson, Abbott of Bury, as a spiritual retreat for the monks farming the land. When it passed into the hands of the Bacon and then the Holt families, it was extended to baronial size. Queen Elizabeth visited it in 1577. Later, in about 1770, Rowland Holt rebuilt the house and had the gardens laid out by Capability Brown, with a huge 45 acre lake. It became one of the greatest estates in the country. Holt also financed major church restructuring, with a tower built from bricks from Woolpit. There are monuments to Sir Nicholas Bacon and his wife Anne. Thomas Wolsey, later Cardinal, was instituted at Redgrave in 1506.

The village sign, erected in 1983, incorporates much of this with one side centre panel depicting the 14th.C. church, former mill, destroyed by fire in 1924 and an ancient barn now converted into cottages. To the left is a ship's/prayer/sexton's bell, and to the right an elegant pipe organ, commemorating the Hart family, who built an organ for Mendlessohn.

Below there are quoits and a clenched hand with three butts behind. This is possibly a connection with Anne Butts whose daughter Anne married Nicholas, Lord Keeper to Elizabeth I and brother of Francis Bacon, also depicting village sports of old. The 'fire' in the hoop could denote Wolsey dying at the stake. The Bacon family is remembered with the pig, decorated by arrows, which tops the sign on each side, again above a horizontal barber-like pole, the motif picked up again in the designs on the spandrel panels.

On the reverse side, under the boar, the central panel shows Redgrave's two rivers, the Little Ouse and the Waveney, which meet in a strange phenomenon. It looks like one river, but here is the source of both, each arising from a spring and each flowing in the opposite direction from the other. This shows Redgrave Fen, the nature reserve, with a variety of wildlife, birds to one side, snake to the other. The fen is home to the rare and the largest spider, the raft spider, shown across the water; fungi, rare lizards and other creatures. There are men cutting sedge, digging for peat. Below the place-name, the spandrel panels show to the left the monks on the river, explained above and to the right ducks on the fen.

Erected in 1983, this attractive sign incorporates much local history, in a fun/pun way, giving the visitor scope to puzzle it out. It stands on the village Green, known as The Knoll.

STONHAM PARVA

Stonham Parva, or Little Stonham, was listed in the Domesday Book as Stanham, meaning 'a stony place'. It has an unusual sign, in that it hangs from the side of the post. A centre oblong is surmounted by a magpie within a crown-shaped cage. This refers to the Magpie Inn, with its live magpie in a cage and its unusual 16th.C pub sign, stretching the whole width across the road, with posts at either end. In the 1970s it had to be temporarily moved to allow the passage of the tiny thatched Mustard Pot Cottage, moved on a lorry from Mendlesham to Bosmere Mill.

As with the sign at Earl Stonham, the coach and horses refer to the fact that the A140 was an important road between Ipswich and Norwich in olden days, when this was the only mode of transport. The typography of the placename under the carriage enhances the sign and links nicely with the wrought iron decoration around it.

LAVENHAM

The unusual sign, made from Suffolk oak and timber taken from Lavenham's oldest house, was designed and carved by Neil Rutherford. Erected straight onto a two-tiered brick base. It was made to commemorate the 70th. Anniversary of Lavenham W.I. 1919-1990. The top panel contains the carved place-name, with three panels below.

The top section features, on the left, the arms of the De Vere family, Earls of Oxford and Lords of the Manor of Lavenham; Top right: Arms of the Springs, wealthy medieval cloth merchants.

Below is a carving of the Tudor Rose.

The centre panel shows a weaver, with his loom, to honour the wealthy wool trade of the town in past times. Wool was dyed here, coining the phrase, 'dyed in the wool'. The bottom panel shows the famous and ancient Guildhall of Corpus Christi, the showpiece of Lavenham. Given to the residents for perpetuity, and now administered by the National Trust, meetings are still held there. The sign is situated on a green near the Church, which can be seen for miles around because it is graced by the highest tower in the country. Mostly rebuilt at the end of the 15th. century, rich cloth merchants donated huge sums towards it, giving it cathedral-like proportions.

Lavenham is on the A1141 and in 1086, the Domesday Book shows the town well-populated, with two manors, church, vineyard, and Aubrey De Vere, brother-in-law of William the Conqueror.

Poet and composer Edward, the 17th. Earl, was at the Court of Elizabeth I and has been thought by some to have been the real author of Shakespeare's plays. The beautiful timber-framed houses, with pastel-washed walls, built by the rich merchants, makes Lavenham famous today. The Market Place, Market Cross, ancient street pattern, buildings, have never been disturbed, giving a fine medieval showplace, which is lived in today. Lavenham also boasted the first sugar beet factory in the country, but that was short-lived due to a fire!

WALDRINGFIELD

Waldringfield overlooks the River Deben, south of Woodbridge. Spelt the same in 950 A.D., its name means 'open land of family/followers of a man called Waldere'.

The wrought-iron sign was made by Mr. E. Jacobs of The Forge, Kirton. It depicts sailing, a popular occupation off Waldringfield. The Anglo-Saxon crown of the chief, Waldhere, surmounts the place-name above.

The design is surrounded by a curled sea monster, the bones of which were found off the local coast. It is related to local deposits of coprolite, (believed to be the fossilised faeces of Mesozoic reptiles) The date, 1977, when the sign was erected to celebrate the Silver Jubilee of Queen Elizabeth II, is stencilled on the serpent's body. The sign, designed by Audrey Fitzjohn is set in an attractive stone circle on a shingle base.

LIDGATE

Lidgate, on the B1063. was termed Litgata in the Domesday Book, meaning 'place at the swing gate'. The village sign, situated at Orchard Close, depicts the Abbot of Bury St. Edmunds monastery, John of Lidgate, whose medieval birthplace, Suffolk House in the village is wonderfully preserved. John is standing in front of the lake, with the church in the background. The church, adapted by the Normans, is on a ridge, built in the bailey of the former castle. The sign is a pastiche design.

On the post a plaque records the award of the Best Kept Village, given by Clare R.D.C. in 1966 and 1996. John of Lidgate, born here in 1370, was a poet and translator, aged 30 when Chaucer stopped writing. John carried on making poetry popular, presenting one volume of his work to young Henry VI and another to Warwick the Kingmaker.

The church was already a hundred years old when John was baptised there, and the tower was built around that time. The original font has long since gone, but the chancel, nave aisles and lofty pillars are still the same. The church was built within the earthworks of the former castle, with a few fragments of wall remaining in the churchyard. The castle moat is still there, but now dry.

John was born without a surname, so took the name of his village, although later he signed his writings as the 'Monk of Bury'. It was at the monastery there that he received his education, studying in Oxford and abroad later. He returned after his travels to write at Bury for the rest of his life. He sent his manuscripts to Chaucer, whom he knew and revered, for criticism. He recorded Agincourt, the coronation of Henry VI, wrote the Dance of Death to illustrate the pictures in St. Paul's Cathedral, the story of the Martyrs of St. Albans, as well as poems commissioned by his patrons. He died in 1451 and was buried at Bury St. Edmunds.

RINGSFIELD

The black wrought iron sign is situated at the crossroads of Cromwell Road and Redisham Road. The design was chosen in 1985,but the unveiling did not occur until July 1998, as the finance was raised in stages. Local craftsman gave their skills and financial backing. Hence the sign itself had been up for over 2 years when an attractive brick flower container base was built and planted. Rory Sherriff and Barry Martin made the base and the sign. It was designed by Mary Bannister and features a tower of rings. A Viking called Rhings, who settled in the village and probably gave it its name, is depicted in the centre ring. The name could equally apply to a circular henged monument found in a clearing. Viking remains have been found near the Church, which is some way off. The original village was resettled around the Green, when people moved away from the source of infection during the plague. A small top ring shows the Ringsfield robin, who nested in the lectern of All Saints' Church, Ringsfield in 1949. She was allowed to hatch and bring up her family and has been immortalised in the carving of a new lectern and in the bronze plaque in the porch gates, designed by Mary Moore and made by her husband at Brandeston Forge. A 15th.C. font has various carved figures. The churchyard was enclosed by a ribbon or Serpentine wall, almost gone now. The sign's bottom double ring holds the place name in the lower half.

Ringsfield church has, on the outside north wall, an elaborate marble monument to Princess Caroline Murat, granddaughter of Napoleon's sister, whose second marriage was to the owner of Redisham Hall. A school, shop, Free church, old and new houses are near the sign, clustered around the Green. Redisham Hall is now a Christian Centre. It was built in 1592 by Nicholas Garnys, then rebuilt on its new site in the mid 18th century and remodelled in 1191 for T. de la Garde Grissell, to whom a metal peacock (the sign of eternal life) is incorporated in an art nouveau memorial window.

THE RICKINGHALLS

Called Rikinghale in the 10th.C., meaning a nook of the family/followers of a man called Rica, Rickinghall lies on the A143 Bury St. Edmunds to Diss road. Its village sign, on an attractive cobblestone base, stands in the churchyard of Rickinghall Inferior and each side depicts one part of the village.

The side for Inferior, has its old Saxon Church of St. Mary, with its Norman round tower, later topped with an octagonal belfry. There is the Saxon lady, Britvolda, who farmed nearby and is mentioned in the Domesday book, a copy of which is shown on the opposite bank of the river beneath the church.

On the Rickinghall Superior side, the now redundant church is featured. Also called St. Mary's, it has a Knights Templar's chapel and ancient stone wall seats on each side, the figure of John de Rickinghall, also known as John Fitzjohn, connected with the Knights Templars, who lived at Fitzjohn Manor and was Chancellor of Cambridge University. On the spandrels underneath the Inferior side there is a flint hammer and the Cross of St. John (for the Knights Templars). The W.I. symbol is in the centre, on the post. The local W.I. shared the cost of the sign with the Parish Council. On the Superior side is a picture of the famous Roman snail, found in a nearby pit, and the boar's head, from the Holt-Wilson coat of Arms, flanking the W.I. symbol. The sign was made by Mr. Paul Hilliard of King's Lynn in 1985.

Superior had a Guildhall, a Knights Templars preceptory, a chapel and a mill. Inferior boasted three mills, a maltings and a school for young ladies, architecturally important, the largest Common in Suffolk, an Elizabethan house, brought in sections from Stowmarket, and a moated farmhouse where the Tyrell family lived. During the 16th.C. a Tyrell was beheaded for the murder of the Princes in the Tower. The publishing Hamlyn Brothers and Basil Brown, archeologist who discovered the Saxon ship burial site at Sutton Hoo, lived here. A time capsule is buried in the sign's base.

STOWUPLAND

'Stow' means 'Place of assembly' or 'holy place', and this derivative of Stowmarket, probably means the land up from Stowmarket. The sign stands on the Stowmarket Road, the B.1115. There was an earlier sign, erected on the Green in 1977 to commemorate the Queen's Silver Jubilee. It showed a white dove, to represent Columbine Hall, the local Manor House, now a farmhouse, a green centre for the village green and flowers to represent the countryside, but it deteriorated and was replaced by the present one, made by Country Craft Studio of Lawshall in 1986.

It is double-sided, with each showing a side of the church. One side also features cricket on the village green and wild flowers above the place-name in black lettering on a white background. The reverse shows the agricultural nature of the village, with wheat ears, partly ploughed stubble field, pile of hay bales and trees. Or does the pile represent the white bricks of Columbine Hall? It is hard to tell.

The crest on the post represents the first family at the Hall, which was built in 1810. A strange ghost story is associated with it. A resident recalls her father living there during 1920s/30s and at 8pm. every evening a strange tapping noise could be heard from the floorboards. Many mice were trapped and caught under the floorboards, but the tapping continued, right through to the next two owners. Sold again, the new resident made alterations. Builders found a hollow place in the wall. It was opened up to reveal a baby's skeleton, walled up for many years. The space was turned into an alcove. No further tapping was ever recorded. Owner Charles Freeman had written in his diary for Sept. 30th. 1825, 'My wife was put to bed at noon of a stillborn male child.', but did not mention a burial. Unchristened babies could not be buried in the churchyard. Did Charles bury his little one in the wall at 8pm that night? We shall never know!

REDISHAM
(Picture Back Cover)

Redisham is on the A145, the Halesworth to Beccles road. An attractive new sign was erected in December 1997. Predominantly blue and gold, the main feature is an open book, to commemorate the life and work of local author Adrian Bell, who lived at The Old Vicarage, nearby. On the right-hand page of the book there is an apple tree, relating to Silverley, in Adrian Bell's well-known book, *The Apple Orchard*. Adrian's son Martin, a television news reporter, who was born there, made national headlines in the 1997 General Election, standing as an Independant candidate fighting 'sleaze'. He was labelled 'The White Knight', not least because of his white suits. On the left-hand page of the book, the village mill is shown. This, now demolished, used to stand on the site of Mr. T. Seaman's transport business opposite the Old Vicarage. The nameplate is in blue below the book and gold rays of the sun light up the top of the sign.

However, there is more for the discerning eye! This is a double-sided sign with a practical purpose. With the sign faces positioned in front of the post, a natural box is made between the two sides. If you look carefully at the 'door' of the mill, you will find that it is indeed a hole! It is hoped that local bluetits will nest there. This is an imaginative and natural touch to this beautiful sign, which was unveiled by Redisham's oldest resident, Mrs. Springall. It was paid for by the Parish council and made in Bramfield by Mick Hart.

Redisham has a small church, with very early chancel walls and an extremely rare and tiny Norman doorway. Formerly 'Great Redisham', 'Little Redisham' was a hamlet to the North of Ringsfield Hall, where traces of an early church and a now vanished settlement have been found.

YAXLEY

Yaxley can be found on the old Roman road, the A140 Norwich to Ipswich. Its name is derived from Jacheslea, Domesday book, meaning wood or clearing of the cuckoo. So it is no surprise that this bird features on both sides of the sign, made by Brian Gaze. The cuckoo is perched on an oak bough on one side, with an hourglass above, symbolising the rising sun.

On the reverse, the cuckoo is on top of a sexton's wheel, representing the sun going down. The cuckoo theme is further depicted on the sign with a cuckoo pint plant and cuckoo flowers. There is a river in the background, greenery, trees and corn, denoting the country location of Yaxley.

The sexton's wheel was used for fixing fast days, or maybe for divination, fortune-telling. There is one on the wall of the church nave, where people have queried their fate since the 15th century. Two flat iron wheels, 2' 6" in diameter, revolve on a common axle. Each has 3 strips attached, numbered for the 6 days of Our Lady. As they spun around, the enquirer would grab a string, to find the answer to his enquiry. The Rev. Sewell found the wheel in separate parts in 1867 in a room above the south porch. Exhibited at an archeologists' gathering brought varying theories, but then some lines were discovered, reading:

The Sexton turns the wheel about and bids the stander-by,
To hold the thread whereby he doth, the time and season try.

It was later suggested that the instrument is similar to the Spanish bell-wheels used for Mass. This could well have been its role before the Reformation. There are only two examples of this medieval machine left, the other being in Long Stratton church, Norfolk. Also in the church the hourglass rests in a fine oak stand. This sturdy attractive wooden sign, designed and painted by Peter Lockwood of Belper, Derbyshire, and Robert Bassett of Etwall, Derbyshire, both senior lecturers at Lonsdale College, has been refurbished by Chassis Cab Ltd. of Bury St. Edmunds. The church has a remarkably fine 15th.C. porch, rich in carving, as is the Jacobean pulpit and canopy. In the 19th. century a rector arranged fragments of ancient glass back into the east window. They are said to be from 1199 - 1549, some of the oldest glass in England. Modern Choreographer Sir Frederick Ashton is buried at Yaxley.

INDEX

Bibliography: Suffolk Guide. N.Scarfe.
Suffolk Village Book. Harold Mills
Suffolk Village Book Suffolk W.I.
Suffolk.   Arthur Mee.
Companion Guide to E. Anglia. J. Seymour.
P.O. Directory of Cambridge, Norfolk & Suffolk.